IMAGES
of America

SIGNAL MOUNTAIN

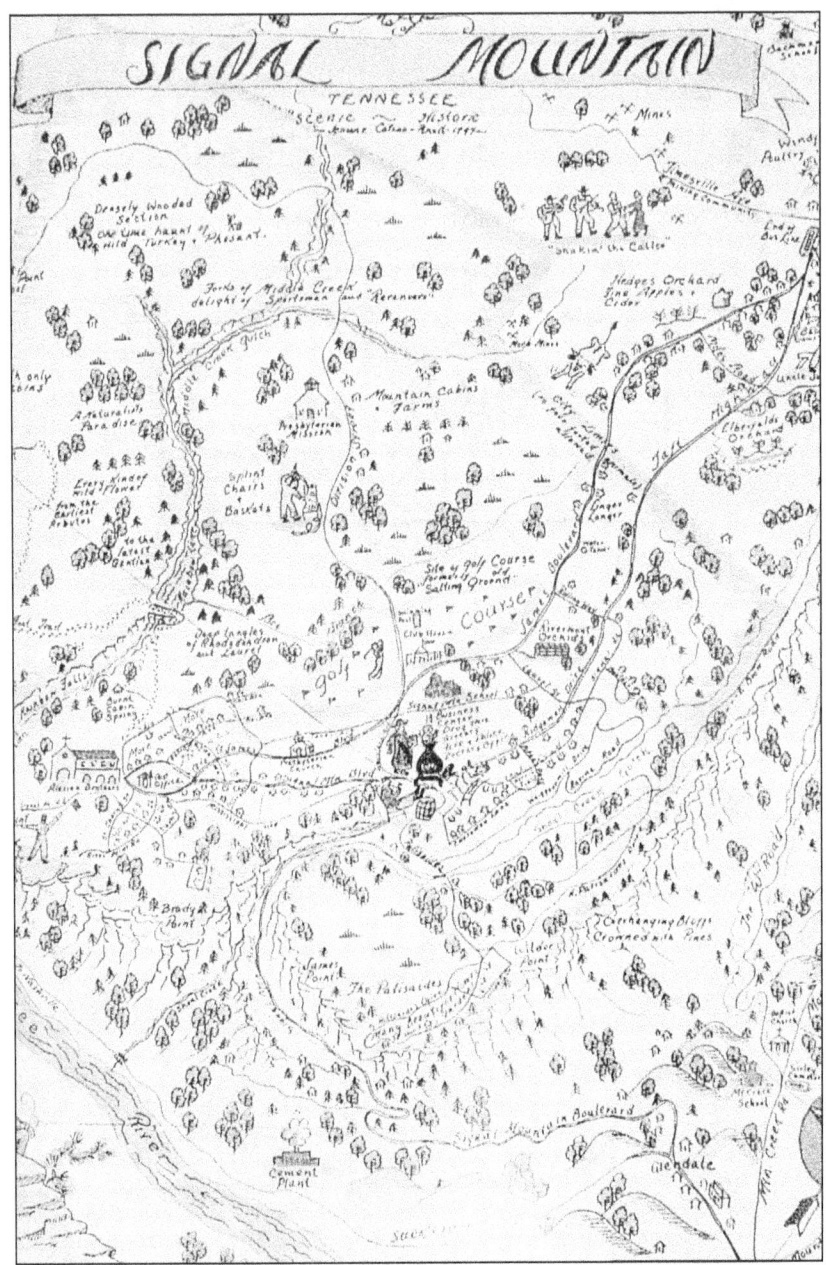

This scenic historic map of Signal Mountain was drawn by Jeanne Catino in 1947. Shown here is the business district near the center of town as well as the Alexian Brothers to the south and a note at the northern town limits that states, "No four footed animals allowed."

ON THE COVER: After the Signal Mountain Inn was built in 1913, a summer recreational area was needed. Rainbow Lake was formed by building a concrete dam across Middle Creek. It was 15 feet deep in places, 1,000 feet long, and 200 feet wide. This playground was surrounded by wild, undisturbed mountain terrain but was only a short walking distance from the hotel. In this idyllic setting, boating and diving into the icy water were favorite pastimes. This photograph was taken before 1920. (Chattanooga–Hamilton County Bicentennial Library.)

IMAGES
of America

SIGNAL MOUNTAIN

Mary Scott Norris
and Priscilla N. Shartle

Copyright © 2008 by Mary Scott Norris and Priscilla N. Shartle
ISBN 978-1-5316-3399-8

Published by Arcadia Publishing
Charleston, South Carolina

Library of Congress Catalog Card Number: 2007942674

For all general information contact Arcadia Publishing at:
Telephone 843-853-2070
Fax 843-853-0044
E-mail sales@arcadiapublishing.com
For customer service and orders:
Toll-Free 1-888-313-2665

Visit us on the Internet at www.arcadiapublishing.com

One of the people whose family left the city for the mountain around 1910 to escape the yellow fever epidemic was Charles E. James. His company, the Mountain Land Company, purchased 4,400 acres of land at Signal Point. One of his first undertakings was the construction of Signal Mountain Boulevard, which led from the bottom of the mountain to the site of the Signal Mountain Inn at Signal Point. From 1912 to 1934, the road also contained the streetcar line to the inn. The Signal Mountain development began as an extension of the popular inn. Soon, due to rapid developments in transportation technology, Signal Mountain became a place of permanent residence. The Town of Signal Mountain was chartered on April 4, 1919. Charles E. James, Fred A. Bryon, and E. M. Ellsworth were elected commissioners. James was selected mayor.

Contents

Acknowledgments		6
Introduction		7
1.	The Early Years	9
2.	C. E. James: Building a Town	15
3.	Scenic Beauty	27
4.	A Town Blossoms	35
5.	Taking Care of Business	49
6.	People	71
7.	Schools and Churches	85
8.	Organizations	107
References		127

Acknowledgments

Mary Scott wishes to express a special appreciation to Mr. and Mrs. William Close (Sarah and Bill) for all the great stories and for their trust and hospitality. My thanks go to Mrs. Hugh Garner (Marilyn), Mrs. John Goss (Nancy), Mrs. Richard Shellabarger (Dot), Mr. Robert Wagner, and Mr. John C. Wynne. To Pris: she is so glad you did the computer work, because neither she nor her computer would have withstood the task. Thank you so much for your expertise! Thanks also to the Town of Signal Mountain Library, Mrs. Louis Glendenning (Karin); the Chattanooga–Hamilton County Bicentennial Library, Karen Myrick and Jim Reece; and the Chattanooga History Center, Brittany Westbrook. Love and thanks go to her children and grandchildren for their support and humor.

Pris would like add her thanks to all the people that Mary Scott mentioned. In addition, she would like to add her appreciation to Lucia Parker Hopper of the *Signal Mountain Mirror* for technical support; Helen Wilson (Mrs. Frank) for loving kindness; the women of the literature department who told her their stories and shared their scrapbooks; and Ellis Smith, great-grandson of a Walden's Ridge pioneer family, for his remarkable ability to look at a picture taken over 70 years ago and be able not only to identify the people and the place, but also tell a story about it and then not hesitate to help when asked. To Mary Scott, she offers her gratitude in your gift of the history of this town and your desire to share the love you have for it by writing this book with her. It was your hard work as assistant librarian organizing the historical files that laid the foundation for this book. Finally she wants to thank her family for their love and patience, especially her dear husband, Mark, for helping her stay balanced and keep her sense of humor.

Together we want to thank Maggie Bullwinkel at Arcadia Publishing for her encouragement, guidance, and support. We loved the cheerful e-mails! Unless otherwise noted, all images are courtesy of the Signal Mountain Library Archives or the private collection of the authors.

INTRODUCTION

The long plateau known as Walden's Ridge, near the tip end of the Appalachian mountain range, has always beckoned travelers to stay a while and enjoy the quiet woods, rippling streams, and majestic, breathtaking views. In the beginning it was a hunting ground. Wildlife—deer, wild turkeys, and rabbits—was plentiful. Native Americans and pioneers alike enjoyed the abundance of game. With time, animal trails became footpaths, and footpaths became pioneer roads. These roads were eventually widened and, in many cases, are the same roads used today. At the dawn of history, the mound builders arrived, leaving mounds of shells that enable us to trace their steps to the Tennessee River. The Creeks were next, and then came the Cherokees. All of these tribes had their villages near the Tennessee River for drinking, cooking, and navigation. Water meant their very lives. It is said that these early people used what is now Signal Point to signal vital messages.

Walden's Ridge did not escape the War Between the States. There were pockets of Confederate families living on farms, most on the back of the mountain near easier access to the valley. Confederate general Braxton Bragg held Chattanooga, but Union soldiers were on the surrounding plateaus around the city and used Signal Point as a relay station. The Federals kept their horses in a pen near Corral Road. Occasionally a skirmish took place between the two sides. Col. John Thomas Wilder was waiting for his chance to take the city. This did occur, and after the war was over, General Wilder came back, having been promoted, purchased the same spot, and built a home where he displayed his medals.

During the 1800s, there were yellow fever and cholera epidemics that took many lives. The worst was the yellow fever siege of 1878. It was traced to a steamer from Cuba that docked in New Orleans in May. Swiftly people became infected, and the death toll began to rise in city after Southern city. In Chattanooga, the decision makers thought that the city was not humid enough and the air too fresh for the illness to be a threat. Many of the afflicted were brought to Chattanooga to recuperate. Soon many of the inhabitants became ill, and the more affluent families fled for the mountains surrounding the city. Here they could spend the hot days in a climate that was about 10 degrees cooler than the valley.

As it happened, Charles E. James was among those who came to the mountain to escape illness. He was a man of vision and was enamored with his surroundings. A dream began to form in his mind. In 1885, he bought a parcel of land near Signal Point, named it Signal Point City, and put lots up for sale. There were problems, and the idea was postponed. One reason could have been that transportation to this remote area was difficult. By 1913, James had brought the electric line up the front of the mountain and had built the Signal Mountain Inn. This formerly isolated area became easily accessible and forever changed.

James finished the golf club in 1918, and this was the catalyst that brought about the chartering of the town. Farm animals often rested idly on the greens and on private lawns. On April 4, 1919, the Town of Signal Mountain was chartered. The first business was to hire a man with a saddle horse to round up strays and impound them on Carlin Street.

Signal Mountain would not have evolved in this idyllic way without benefactors and community-minded clubs. Walter A. Marr was a brilliant and altruistic citizen without whom this mountain settlement would not be the same. He was an automobile magnate who was a key player at the beginning of the industry. His peers were Henry Ford, Walter Chrysler, Billy Durant, and the Dodge brothers. He was a devout person and a family man and helped in every way possible to make Signal Mountain a nurturing place for children to grow. Realizing that there was a need for a spiritual haven, he built Marr Chapel, and he and his wife presented it to people of all faiths; it is now part of the Signal Mountain Presbyterian Church.

Mr. and Mrs. Z. Cartter Patten II (Elizabeth) gave the town two large tracts of land now known as Coolidge Parkway, named for a young hero, Sgt. Charles Coolidge, who was awarded the Congressional Medal of Honor for extraordinary valor in World War II. Many times, the Pattens made a donation to help when there was a need in the town. Mr. Patten penned *Signal Mountain and Walden's Ridge*, often called the most accurate history ever written about the mountain. They built a lovely home known as Longview and resided there part of the year. Their love for the mountain was always evident.

The Garden Club of Signal Mountain and the Community Guild planted dogwoods up and down the streets of the town starting in 1928. Every spring, when the dogwoods bloom, locals are thankful for these industrious workers of long ago. The beauty of the landscape is one of the primary reasons people have moved to the mountain over the decades. Some fun events are the Fourth of July picnic and fireworks and the Labor Day barbecue. These events have been presented by the Lions Club and the Community Guild. There is a book sale at the library.

The first public school, the Signal Mountain Grammar School, was for grades one through eight. The wonderful little school produced many scholars. The building continues to be used for the Mountain Arts Community Center and holds classes pertaining to the arts.

One of the first grocery stores was Morgan's Store. Outside were bags of feed for animals and chickens, and firewood was for sale. Through the double doors, the interior was very dark and mysterious in the eyes of a child, with only a few light bulbs hanging down from the ceiling. Large barrels contained sweet potatoes, corn, green beans, apples, and nuts. On the counter close to the register were jars of candy of every kind to entice a wide-eyed child. The best surprise was in the basement: a family of six-toed cats.

The first doctors made house calls after office hours. Dr. Wert and Dr. M. L. Langston were early mountain doctors. Dr. Langston, beloved by his patients, had the first office on Signal. His was succeeded by Dr. Archibald Smith III, an excellent physician who has continued ministering to the population even after retirement by volunteering his skills.

This book was not meant to be a concise history of the town of Signal Mountain; we have attempted to give a general picture of the people, places, events, and landmarks in honor of all those who came before us. Many of the special qualities of life, past and present, on Signal Mountain are captured on the following pages. Let's take a tour!

One

THE EARLY YEARS

In 1857, few families lived on Walden's Ridge. There were no incorporated towns. In July 1858, a one-room school, the first schoolhouse in Hamilton County, was built in the Fairmount community. Known as the Old Academy or the Fairmount Academy, the school closed during the Civil War and reopened in 1872. It was made a public school in 1880.

The Fairmount Academy was used as a community center by the Ladies Aid and the PTA, and all elections were held there until it burned in 1946. By then, the Fairmount Elementary School had been built at the corner of Fairmount Road and Anderson Pike. It closed in 1937. Today the Mountain Opry, home to bluegrass music, resides in one of the remaining buildings.

The Union Chapel, also known as "the Little Brown Church," was built in 1908. It was established to serve the community of Summertown, composed of people who spent their summers on the mountaintop. Today it remains a nondenominational church that meets only during the summer months. Located in the town of Walden, it has a long tradition of welcoming men, women, children, and their pets from all over the area.

At the onset of the Civil War, John Thomas Wilder became a private in the army and was promoted to captain on the second day. Soon he advanced to the rank of lieutenant colonel. Wilder distinguished himself in many battles, including Shiloh. Uniquely, he equipped his men with arms. The young officer borrowed the money for new reloading Spencer rifles from an Indiana bank, and the men agreed to pay him back. Wilder positioned his troops for a clear view of the city before the Battle of Chattanooga at the spot pictured below and in the surrounding area. Confederate general Braxton Bragg thought that he was surrounded and left the city. Wilder's men went down the mountain, crossed the river, and planted the first flag. Later, in 1912, General Wilder bought this property and built a large house, which later burned. (Chattanooga History Center.)

Coal mines were located on the bluff overlooking the Tennessee River. This photograph shows a mine shaft and early miners prominent in the early part of Signal Mountain's history. The mines ran underground for miles from the brow on one side of the ridge to the brow overlooking the valley on the other side of the ridge. The coal was soft and plentiful. (Sarah and Bill Close.)

This woman, pictured standing in front of her home in the late 1920s, was typical of the mining community near Edward's Point. Many of these families were poor and had no running water or electricity. Most suffered from black lung disease and depended on their government checks. (Sarah and Bill Close.)

The Federal Military Road dates back to 1864. It is thought to be located at Elks Curve, which is located at first curve in the "S" curve on Signal Mountain Boulevard. Today this curve can be a problem for large trucks coming up the mountain. Just past the curve on the left is the "spaceship" house, a circular, white structure that stands on four legs and has become a local landmark.

A group of people, possibly a family, rests by a water mill as a man stops to talk with them. Everyone knew everyone's name in the early days before the town incorporated. Many families descending from the early miners still live off Edward's Point. (Sarah and Bill Close.)

Before the Chickamauga Dam was built, a significant flood event occurred in Chattanooga every 10 years or so. Most people lived close to the city proper, and even when heavy rains did not bring a flood, the fear was present. The flood of 1917 was the last straw for many families. With the momentum of new homes and budding community life on Signal Mountain, family after family flocked to start a new life, free of the thought of rising waters and subsequent danger and disease. These pictures, taken in 1917, show the flooded streets of downtown Chattanooga. (Chattanooga History Center.)

Two
C. E. James
Building a Town

C. E. James is pictured wearing a white shirt and straw hat in the center of this photograph, which was taken around 1912, when the work crew began construction of Signal Mountain Boulevard. (Chattanooga–Hamilton County Bicentennial Library.)

The date of this picture is unknown but must have been some time before 1912. The highway up the mountain is being cleared before the streetcar tracks were built. The blasted mountain stone was later hand-cut and used to build the Signal Mountain Inn and many of the surrounding homes in Signal Mountain Place. (John C. Wynne.)

Once the highway was cleared and the road firm, progress continued. This photograph shows one of the early roads that lead off Signal Mountain Boulevard, the main road. It shows the higher elevation and cliffs above the road near the top of the ridge. (Sarah and Bill Close.)

This car is being driven down the mountain just after the road was cleared. The photograph was taken some time between 1912 and 1913. The drive up the mountain took 45 minutes. (John C. Wynne.)

This photograph, taken around 1913, shows an aerial view of Walden's Ridge before the incorporation of Signal Mountain. (Chattanooga–Hamilton County Bicentennial Library.)

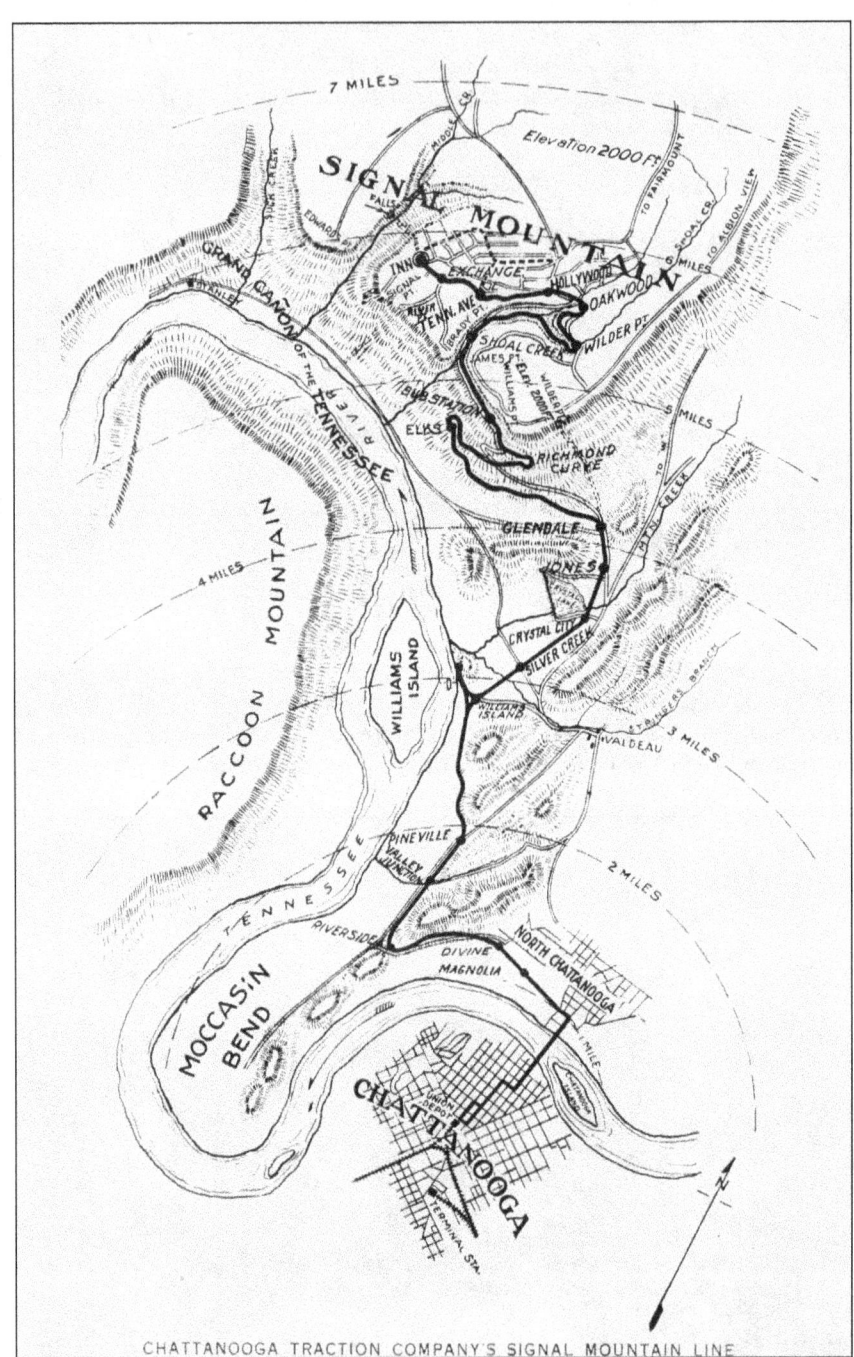

The Chattanooga Traction Company's Signal Mountain Line ran from downtown Chattanooga across the Tennessee River and up Signal Mountain. At the end of the line was the Signal Mountain Inn. Alongside the tracks, an automobile and carriage road was constructed from Chattanooga. Both rides from Chattanooga took 40 minutes. James died in October 1925. Money was collected for the monument to be erected across from James Point at his death to commemorate all the contributions he made to the Chattanooga area. The monument was moved in 1969 to James Park.

The electric car was called a streetcar, not a trolley. The elevation at this point was 1,700 feet. It traveled along Shoal Creek, making its first stop at Wilder Station. It then crossed over Ridgeway Avenue and followed the path up Mississippi Avenue, down Maryland Avenue, stopping at Hollywood Station, and then finally ending at the hotel. (John C. Wynne.)

Signal Mountain Streetcar No. 14 of the Chattanooga Traction Company is pictured around 1915 running alongside a rock face at James Point on Walden's Ridge. (Chattanooga–Hamilton County Bicentennial Library.)

The Signal Mountain Inn was located in Signal Mountain Place and was a handsome, modern, fireproof hotel. It was four stories tall and had hot and cold running water in every room, as well as a telephone. It was referred to as both an inn and a hotel. Saddle horses, carriages, and automobiles were available for rent. It was owned and managed by the Mountain Land Company.

This picture, taken from the Mountain Land Company's book on Signal Mountain Properties, is of the residence of C. E. James in Signal Mountain Place. Located across the street from the inn, the home was used when he visited the mountain.

The dining room at the Signal Mountain Inn was a large room lighted on two sides by rows of large windows commanding views of the main approach to the hotel on one side and the deep Tennessee River gorge toward Rainbow Lake on the other. A unique feature was a separate dining room for children. Prices, as shown on the menu, were considered reasonable. Fresh eggs, milk, and vegetables grown in the inn's own garden were prepared daily, along with every delicacy known. Meals were served from 6:00 a.m. until 10:00 p.m. (Sarah and Bill Close.)

SIGNAL MOUNTAIN HOTEL
Overlooking Chattanooga

Menu

Salads

Chicken, Mayonnaise	.60	Mixed Vegetable	.40
Lobster	.75	French String Bean	.40
Crabmeat	.75	Potato	.30
Shrimp	.60	Cole Slaw	.30
Tomato, Stuffed with Chicken	.60	Celery Slaw	.30
Tomatoes, Sliced	.40	Pear and Cheese	.40
Tomato and Lettuce, Mayonnaise	.40	Pineapple and Cheese	.40
Lettuce, Mayonnaise	.35	Grape Fruit	.50
Lettuce, French Dressing	.35	Mixed Fruit	.60
Lettuce, Russian Dressing	.60	Celery, Apple, Nut	.50
Lettuce, Roqueford Dressing	.60	Celery, Apple, Cheese	.50
Salmon	.50	Spring Salad	.40
Tuna	.50	Mexican Salad	.40
Asparagus, Vinaigrette	.50	Cottage Cheese and Pepper	.40

Served with Toasted Crackers

Sandwiches

Signal Mountain Club	.75	Lettuce, Mayonnaise	.25
Chicken	.50	Lettuce, Tomato, Bacon	.40
Chicken Salad	.50	Lettuce, Tomato	.30
Deviled Ham and Chicken	.40	Imported Swiss Cheese	.30
Baked Ham	.40	American Cream Cheese	.30
Broiled Ham	.50	Philadelphia Cream Cheese	.30
Broiled Bacon	.40	Cream Cheese and Honey	.30
Smoked Tongue	.40	Pimento Cheese	.30
Roast Beef	.50	Cheese Salad	.30
Imported Frankfurter	.40	Roqueford Cheese	.30
Fried Egg	.30	Caviar	.50
Deviled Egg	.30	Pineapple	.30
French Sardine	.40	Peanut Butter	.25

Toasted 10c Extra
Served on Rye, Whole Wheat or White Bread

Drinks

Coffee—Small Pot	.15	Half and Half	.25
Cup	.10	Lemonade	.25
Iced	.15	Orange Ade	.25
Tea	.15	Spanish Chocolate	.25
Iced Tea	.15	Canada Dry	.35
Milk	.10	Coca-Cola	.10
Buttermilk	.10	Budweiser	.25

The lobby of the Signal Mountain Hotel was not only used by guests but also for special occasions by the residents in the community. Weddings, luncheons, Scout functions, teas, and an annual Easter egg hunt leading out to the grounds from the lobby were among the many uses. (Sarah and Bill Close.)

The swimming pool at the Signal Mountain Inn was originally just for men. It was the first swimming pool in the town but was not open to the public. This photograph shows boys and girls sharing the pool, with their mothers sitting under the pavilion. The man standing on the side is probably the lifeguard or swimming instructor, as this could have been a swimming lesson offered by the hotel. (Sarah and Bill Close.)

Horseback riding was available to guests at the Signal Mountain Inn. Beautiful bridle paths were found in the woods near the Signal Mountain Hotel. On this well-worn path, riders rode side-by-side enjoying the natural beauty of the area. A favorite spot to see the Tennessee River for guests at the Signal Mountain Inn was Signal Point. Hiking and horseback riding were available to all guests. (Sarah and Bill Close.)

Opening
DANCE TONIGHT!
in the
HANGAR
9:30 to 12:30
Van Arsdale's
Signal Mountain Hotel Orchestra

The first dance in the Hangar at the Signal Mountain Hotel was held Saturday, May 18, 1935. People came from off the mountain as well as from the town of Signal Mountain to join the guests at the hotel dancing to live music performed by George Van Arsdale's Orchestra, a band from Chattanooga. Van Arsdale's wife, Jean, was the organist at the Tivoli Theater in Chattanooga. Every Saturday night from 9:30 to 12:30 between the beginning of May and Labor Day, people enjoyed the music. The cost—$1 per couple—was collected at the door. The Hangar was "air-cooled" by a giant exhaust fan.

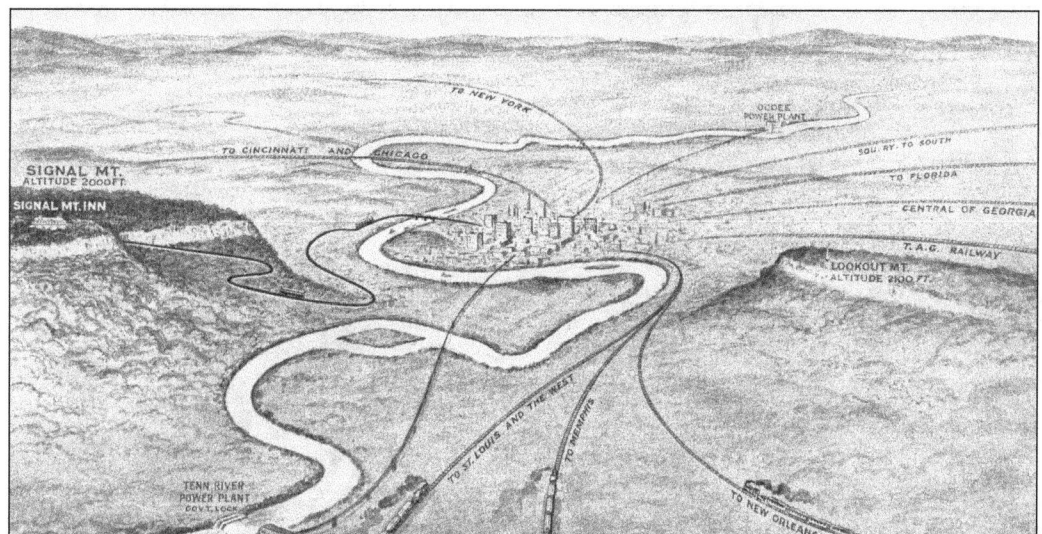
Signal Mountain and the Signal Mountain Inn are seen in this map created by the Chattanooga Traction Company to advertise how accessible the inn was to the rest of the United States. Chattanooga was considered the gateway to and the railroad center of the South.

This view of the Signal Mountain palisades from across the river shows the cement plant, which is still located on what is now Suck Creek Road. This plant was built by the Mountain Land Company to surface the road coming up the mountain, build the hotel, and then was used to build the streets and houses surrounding the hotel. (Sarah and Bill Close.)

The small area known as Burnt Cabin Springs near Rainbow Lake was located along the road between the golf course and the lake. Known as the "Queen of all Waters" for the cure of stomach, liver, and kidney troubles, the mineral waters were near the Signal Mountain Inn. This type of "epsomia" water was present in abundance and became popular with the guests of the inn. The burnt cabin for which the springs are named was built by prospector D. B. Collins, who was on the mountain looking for the coal first mined here in 1890. Minnie Carruth reported in the April 1931 issue of the *Garden Club Exchange*, "In a friendly rivalry, members of the Signal Mountain Community Guild and members of the Signal Mountain Garden Club united in a concentrated effort to clean up the springs and the path between the springs and Rainbow Lake. They exposed the gorgeous wildflowers, native shrubs, ferns and beautiful old weathered stones. This common interest gripped the hearts of the women of Signal Mountain."

Three

SCENIC BEAUTY

This photograph, titled "Dogwood Blossoms of Signal Mountain," was taken by Herbert Jackson and featured in *The Volunteer Gardener*, the official publication of the Tennessee Federation of Garden Clubs, in the spring of 1958. The thousands of dogwoods, redbuds, and flowering shrubs that contributed to the beauty of the community were not there by accident of nature. They were planted by garden clubs, the Signal Mountain Community Guild, and individual citizens over a long period of time. Lena Givens led the program and stayed behind it relentlessly. To support the effort, the Annual Dogwood Festival, sponsored by the Signal Mountain Civic League, was a tremendous undertaking that lasted a week and included at its height, teas; tours of gardens and homes; the Dogwood Luncheon; a flower show; and a Junior Garden Club spring flower show at the Signal Mountain Grammar School. It ended with a coronation ball at the club. (Signal Mountain Community Guild Archives.)

Probably the most sought-after view by artists and the most requested scene, this view of Williams Island on the Tennessee River is seen from James Point. (Sarah and Bill Close.)

This c. 1917 photograph shows another view from James Point, this time facing the city of Chattanooga. In the distance is Williams Island. The Tennessee River can be seen below with Elder Mountain across the river. (Sarah and Bill Close.)

This photograph, taken around 1942, is of Mushroom Rock, located just above North Suck Creek on the Cumberland Trail just as it descends. The rock is just off West Hassler Road and is considered a favorite sight for hikers in the area. (Chattanooga–Hamilton County Bicentennial Library.)

Middle Creek is one of the main creeks through the town of Signal Mountain. At one time, this creek was dammed to create Rainbow Lake, but now it runs freely. When there are heavy rains in the Hidden Brook neighborhood—called so because of the many hidden brooks—entire front and back yards can swell up with water that flows into Middle Creek. (Sarah and Bill Close.)

This photograph of Wagner Pond, formerly Elberfeld Pond, was taken around 1943. The manmade pond watered the apple orchards that surrounded it. Bob Wagner's grandfather bought the property from the Elberfeld family and later sold a portion to the Hedges family. One day Bob's father, Joe Wagner, came home from school and found his parents in the front yard, holding each other as they watched their home near the pond burn down. The picture of the barn was taken by the Pulitzer prize–winning photographer Robin Hood. It is unknown when the picture was taken, but it was long before the surrounding area was developed. Wagner's Barn is the oldest remaining barn in Signal Mountain, according to the owners. Located on James Boulevard, the barn can still be seen on the hill by the pond. (Bob Wagner.)

This photograph, taken of the cliffs of Walden's Ridge, shows how steep the cliffs were, and one can see Brady Point off in the distance. (Sarah and Bill Close.)

This picture, probably taken around 1920, shows a view of the road up Signal Mountain before there was much development. The road along the edge of the ridge is Signal Mountain Boulevard. The tracks of the electric line are visible. (Sarah and Bill Close.)

On March 3, 1960, Signal Mountain was hit with the worst ice storm in the history of the town. The town was said to look like a shell-shattered battlefield. Four days later, more snow fell, and the National Guard turned away nonresidents. Access up and down the mountain was difficult. Downtown hotels and motels were jammed with stranded residents of the mountain. These photographs show downed power lines near the traffic light and the ice-covered trees that downed them. Ninety percent of the residents on the mountain lost power. Over a 1,000 men battled zero-degree temperatures to repair lines. The post office was closed for two days, but thanks to Bill Smith at the Mountain Service Station, mail service resumed. The storm knocked out 8,110 telephones. The cost of damage was estimated at $5 million. The ice storm took its toll on native trees and plants, but today, little remains of the massive destruction. (Chattanooga–Hamilton County Bicentennial Library.)

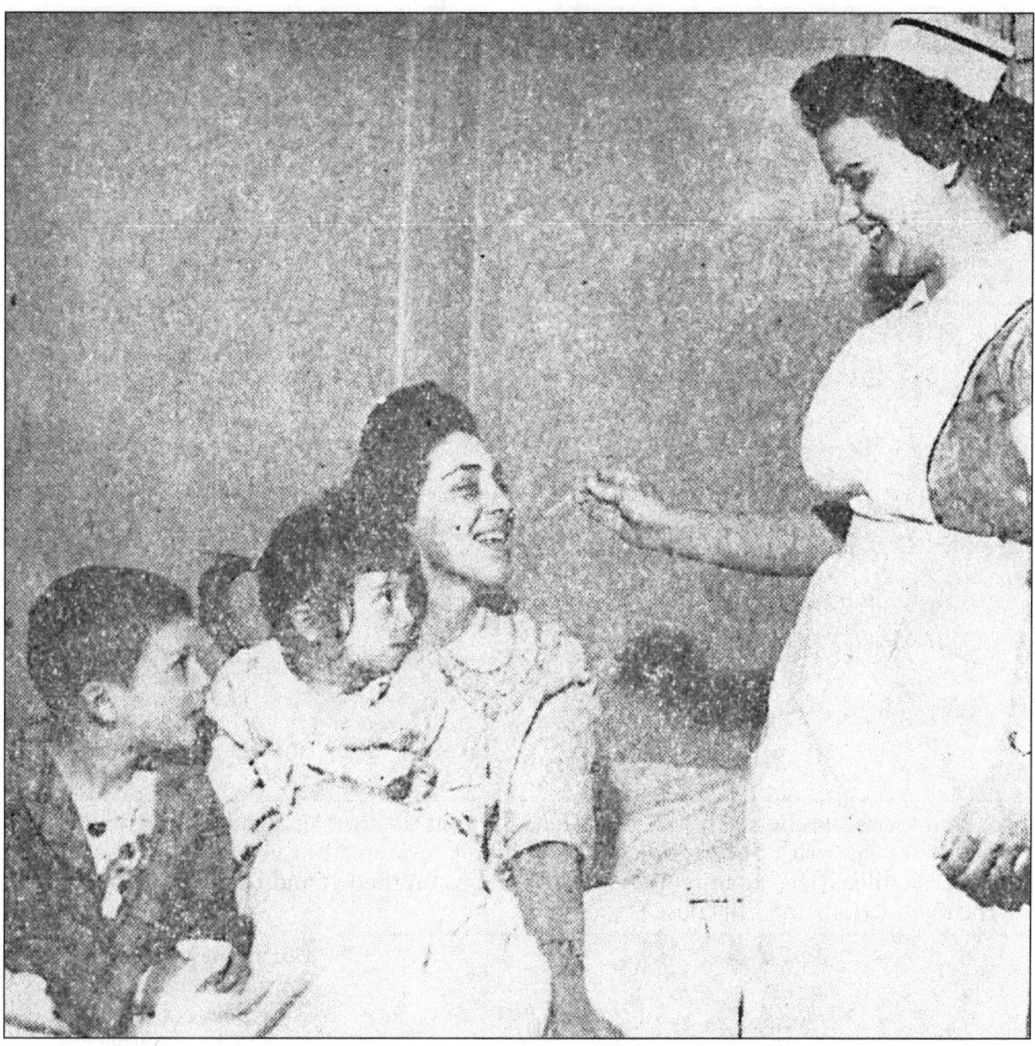

Room was made at Children's Hospital in Chattanooga when Frank W. Atkinson made every effort possible to get his family medical help at the height of the ice storm on March 3, 1960. When the family doctor reached their home, he found Mrs. Atkinson with pneumonia and the other three members of the family with the flu. There was no power, and the telephone lines were down. The doctor made it back to the fire hall, and an ambulance was summoned. It took the drivers over 45 minutes to get down the mountain, having to stop often to remove fallen trees. Frank Atkinson became the first adult male to be admitted to the hospital, and Hilda Atkinson became the first adult female to be admitted since 1938, when the hospital stopped its obstetrics services. The doctor on call said, "Emergency conditions demand emergency solutions." Pictured, from left to right, are Andy, age six; Hillaine, age four; Mrs. Atkinson; and Jean Ann Voorhees, student nurse. (Signal Mountain Community Guild Archives.)

This brow view from the north side of Walden's Ridge in the town of Signal Mountain Palisades section looks east, with Spring Valley or Mountain Creek area to the left, and way off in the distance the Blue Ridge mountains of North Carolina on the left and Lookout Mountain high on the right. (Sarah and Bill Close.)

Because temperatures on the mountaintop are up to 10 degrees cooler than those in the valley, native plants and trees survive best there, but thanks to the efforts of the Signal Mountain Community Guild and garden clubs in the town, thousands of dogwood trees were planted over many years to blend in with the wild dogwoods already present. Unfortunately, a blight in the late 20th century killed many of the oldest trees, especially those that lined James Boulevard. (Chattanooga–Hamilton County Bicentennial Library.)

Four

A Town Blossoms

By 1913, the Signal Mountain Inn was complete, and the electric cars were running up and down the mountain. By 1918, the Signal Mountain Golf Course was complete. The golf course was called "the Links." Since the time of pioneer settlers, farmers had brought their livestock to Walden's Ridge in the spring and left them until fall to fatten them up. Soon cattle and pigs were found in groups on the greens. They also showed up on private lawns and were difficult to relocate. On April 14, 1919, the Town of Signal Mountain received its charter, and the first order of business was to outlaw animals on the golf course. By 1925, two hundred homes had been built, most within a few blocks of the Signal Mountain Inn and golf course. (Sarah and Bill Close.)

This is a picture looking up Carlin Street (center) from Ridgeway Avenue, taken in the 1930s. The land on the left side of the street was called the "Old Pen" because loose cows, pigs, and horses found roaming around town were kept here. Residents would come to the pen, pay a fine, and collect their stray animals. It is now the location of the Signal Mountain Cleaners. (John C. Wynne.)

Although the picture is somewhat blurry, this car has just left Signal Mountain Boulevard and is turning to go down the mountain. It was probably taken in the early 1930s and is thought to have been taken from a streetcar as it was passing over Ridgeway Drive, which explains the blurred photograph. (John C. Wynne.)

A streetcar passes 410 Wood Street, located near the Old Pen. This photograph was taken in 1924. (John C. Wynne.)

The date of this picture is unknown. It shows a streetcar traveling up the snow-covered mountain. What is most interesting is the clear view of all the electric poles and lines that were connected to the cars. It is said that once the streetcar arrived at the hotel, the conductor would get out and put the pole at the other end of the car to go back down the mountain. (John C. Wynne.)

This intersection is Signal Mountain Boulevard and Mississippi Avenue. Workers are paving the road. The streetcar tracks on Mississippi Avenue lead to the Signal Mountain Inn in the direction of Brady Point, as the sign points on the utility pole. Signal Mountain Boulevard crossed Main Avenue (now James Boulevard), made a loop, and ended at this spot. The house on the left was one of the first homes built after the hotel and is made of hand-carved stone. According to the current owners, Mr. and Mrs. Phil Johnson (Allison), there were at least four other homes designed and built like this one at the time. Although it cannot be confirmed that the building materials were local, it is obvious that indigenous hardwood and limestone were used in the Craftsman-style bungalows found throughout the neighborhood. (John C. Wynne.)

Mr. and Mrs. Foster V. Brown's home was built on Main Avenue in 1914 and is the best example of a natural bungalow. Later it became the summer home of Mrs. E. Y. Chapin (Elise Hutcheson), who is pictured here. The home was well known for her beautiful wild-flower gardens. In addition to homes, cottages owned by the Mountain Land Company were rented, and lots were sold for between $500 and $2,000.

Today this is the home of Mr. and Mrs. Pat Kelly (Kathleen), and it is located at the corner of James Boulevard and Tennessee Avenue. Many of the homes still stand and are located in the area of Signal Mountain now known as "Old Towne." In 2005, the U.S. Department of the Interior's National Park Service listed the area in the National Register of Historic Places as the Signal Mountain Historic District.

The residence of Karl D. Hawk on Main Avenue is pictured in the Mountain Land Company's book, which states that sites for either summer or permanent homes were provided for sale by the company. The Hawks later turned their home into a bed-and-breakfast called the Hawk's Nest. Today their daughter, Mary Nelle Burke, lives in her family home on what is now called James Boulevard, across the street from the Signal Mountain Presbyterian Church. At one time, there were several little houses on the property, including one shaped like a pagoda. It had been a ticket booth in downtown Chattanooga. According to Mr. Hawk's granddaughter, Janis Burke Speck, her grandfather moved it up the mountain, glassed in the walls, installed plumbing and electricity, and rented it out. It still stands on the property.

Two photographs taken around 1937 show how proud the Signal Mountain Fire and Police Department was of its engines. In the first picture, standing beside a Seagraves fire engine, a Reo fire engine, and a Chevrolet police car in front of the Signal Mountain Fire and Police Station are, from left to right, Chief Charles A. Brown, Arnold F. "Slim" Varner, Raymond Varner, Norris Smedley, and Harve Tallent. In the second photograph, from left to right, are Raymond Varner, Slim Varner, Chief Charles A. Brown, Harve Tallent, and Norris Smedley. (John C. Wynne.)

This picture was taken in the early 1940s, just after Taft Highway was built in 1938. On the left is the Gulf gas station, which is next door to the Signal Mountain Fire and Police Station. The road on the right is Signal Mountain Boulevard. (John C. Wynne.)

These Gulf gas pumps were located at the Signal Mountain Fire and Police Station. The picture was probably taken in the early 1930s. Chief Charles Brown sold gas, cold drinks, and snacks here as a side business. (John C. Wynne.)

Chief Charles A. Brown sits on a Reo fire truck in front of the Signal Mountain Fire and Police Station. The picture was probably taken in the late 1920s. (John C. Wynne.)

Chief Brown stands in front of the streetcar trestle over Carlin Street. This picture was probably taken in the late 1920s or early 1930s. Carlin Street was across the street from the fire and police station. (John C. Wynne.)

The town barber was George Gouvista. Here he is pictured with Chief Charles A. Brown. The Signal Mountain Barber and Beauty Parlor was located in the same building as Morgan's Store. Everybody called him "George, My Barber." In the second picture are, from left to right, Elmer Handley, Mitchell Smith, Marvin Setliffe, Homer Pickett, and Charles Wicks at Morgan's Store. This picture was taken around 1940. The building, which was owned by J. C. Morgan, was on Signal Mountain Boulevard. Morgan's store was on the far left, and in the middle was a little restaurant that served the best hamburgers according to longtime residents. Homer Pickett ran the restaurant, and Marie Worlen ran the beauty parlor, which was on the far right along with the barbershop. (John C. Wynne.)

Wright's Market was located on Ridgeway Avenue, across the street from the Signal Mountain Fire and Police Station on the land that is now James Park. This photograph was probably taken in the 1940s according to Ellis Smith, who is pictured in the center of the second photograph wearing a white apron. This was his first job. Pictured from left to right in front of the grocery are Thomas L. Wright, owner of the market; Russell Hicks; Ellis Smith; Joel Wright; and Arthur Sharp. (John C. Wynne.)

Bill Smith (left), Homer Edmondson (center), and Norris Smedley sit in front of Smedley's Texaco station in the early 1940s. Smedley's Texaco was the only gas station in town other than the Gulf at the fire and police station.

Smedley's Texaco was located on the corner of Signal Mountain Boulevard and Mississippi Avenue. Today Mountain Service Imports, an import-car repair shop, is in the building that once was Smedley's. This photograph was also probably taken in the early 1940s. (John C. Wynne.)

The first Signal Mountain Post Office was located on the corner of Signal Mountain Boulevard and James Boulevard. In 1946, Ester Whitman was the part-time clerk. Preston Guthrie was the city carrier, and Ellis Smith Jr. was the rural letter carrier, having been hired originally as a Christmas assistant. He remained rural letter carrier until he retired in 1980 without missing one day of work during his career.

Gordon Holderness was the regular carrier when the post office was moved to Ridgeway Avenue in 1954. Harry L. Robinson was the postmaster. It then moved across the street from Signal Plaza Shopping Center and remained there until 1996. Naomi Thurman was the clerk. The post office moved once again to its present site, pictured here, on Ridgeway Avenue.

Signal Mountain Boulevard, the road coming up the mountain, became Ridgeway Avenue at this intersection. Ridgeway Avenue extended as far as Rolling Way, which was considered the end of town at the time. The corner of Ridgeway Avenue and Signal Mountain Boulevard was the center of town by the 1930s, with the town hall and fire and police station on one corner and the pharmacy on the other. (John C. Wynne.)

This picture of the Signal Mountain Pharmacy, located at the corner of Palisades Drive and Ridgeway Avenue, was probably taken in the early 1940s. "Doc" Smith was the druggist, and his wife ran the store. They had a very popular soda fountain with grilled sandwiches, fountain drinks, ice cream, and milk shakes. In 1952, Dr. Marvin Woodard, the first dentist in the town, opened an office in this building. (John C. Wynne.)

Five

TAKING CARE OF BUSINESS

Charles B. Adams served as superintendent for the Town of Signal Mountain from 1929 to 1959. At a ceremony on September 4, 1950, Adams was honored for his service to the community. A watch was presented to him during the picnic held at the club. Former mayor Joe Richardson recalled how Adams "got out and worked day and night" during the Depression. In April 1981, Mayor Marion Summerville accepted a new flagpole on behalf of the Town of Signal Mountain. Presenting the flagpole to the town was Mrs. Hugh Garner (Marilyn), president of the Signal Mountain Civic Council. The new Signal Mountain flagpole was dedicated at Adams Square at the corner of Carlin Street and Ridgeway Avenue. Just below the flag, embedded in mountain stone, sits this monument honoring Charlie Adams.

The Palisades section is a beauty to behold. To stand at the brow and look out onto the valley toward Chattanooga is a wonderful sight. Residents wanted to live on the brow to benefit from this beautiful view, and so neighborhoods grew up at the south end of town. This photograph shows Lookout Mountain in the distance, in the center of the photograph. (Sarah and Bill Close.)

This photograph shows South Palisades Drive at the first stages of development, before construction of houses began. Palisades Drive begins at Ridgeway Drive on the same corner as the pharmacy and the fire and police station. The road was laid out and the trees were clear-cut so houses could be built. (Sarah and Bill Close.)

The first real neighborhood for permanent residents was located in the Palisades section. This home on South Palisades Drive was built in 1929–1930. The photograph shown was taken in 1934, when it was owned by Tom S. Thach, who bought it in April of that year, shortly before his marriage to Mary Frances McGhee on June 28. He paid $4,000, a greatly reduced price because it was the middle of the Depression. (Sarah and Bill Close.)

Homes built at this time were much larger and more expensive than those built in what is now called Old Towne, near the hotel. Many of the Palisades homes were more English Tudor in design, as shown here. This particular house had three bedrooms, two baths, a living room, a dining room, a butler's pantry, a servant's room with bath, hardwood floors, and a garage. It sold for $16,000 new. (Sarah and Bill Close.)

Members of the recreation board, set up under a state enabling act, were Mrs. J. C. Heindel (Mary), Dr. M. F. Langston, Alfred E. Smith, Paul Mathes, and Mrs. Howard Sears. In 1950, the board set a goal of $4,500 to be raised. Heading up the fund drive are, from left to right, (first row) Mrs. O. M. Derryberry (Kay), Andy Nardo, and Martha Nelson; (second row) Alfred E. Smith, R. T. Faucette Jr., Robert McEwan, and William E. Keck Jr.

Chick Thorington, instructor at the Signal Mountain swimming pool, is shown with boys at the pool in July 1952. The pool was located behind the Signal Mountain Golf and Country Club on James Boulevard. The boys, from left to right, are Preston Hamilton, David Oha, Steve Watson, George Derryberry, Andy Cope, Terry Walker, Gordon Cope, Buddy Lanston, Chris McEwan, Rickey Bohr, George Seiters, and Dick Rogers.

In September 1953, the Signal Mountain Commission, consisting of Mayor Claude Givens, Commissioner Charlie Dodd, and Treasurer Phil Stegall (pictured right) were highly commended. After these public-spirited and capable gentlemen came to office, many worthwhile improvements were made in the town, including improving finances by reducing the bond indebtedness and making money with the new water system, which called for all citizens to say, "Thanks for a good job well done." Pictured from left to right are Shirley Alderman, a local TV personality; Mr. and Mrs. Charles Dodd (Marian); Mrs. L. B. Godfrey (Margaret); and Donald Whithorne, the first president of the Signal Mountain Lions Club. This photograph, taken by Phil Truex, was for a press release.

Water for the town of Signal Mountain had to be piped up from the bottom of the ridge. The path along which the pipes were laid was used by local citizens as a footpath down the mountain. This path was called "the Dog Hole." Longtime residents who used the path knew exactly where it began on the brow off South Palisades Drive.

Hedges Apple Orchard was located on James Boulevard. The Hedges family bought the property from the Wagner family in 1921. The pond between the two properties was used to water the apple orchards. According to Mary Hedges, their daughter, when the family sold the land to a contractor, he suggested the new neighborhood be called the Orchard. Everyone agreed on the new name. (John C. Wynne.)

This picture was taken in the early 1930s at the later sight of Wright's Food Market, across the street from the Signal Mountain Fire and Police Station. Standing in front of a Seagraves fire engine are, from left to right, Frank Robbins Jr., Frank Robbins Sr., Charles A. Brown with his children in front of him, Norris Smedley, Harve Tallent, Raymond Varner, and Preston Guthrie. (John C. Wynne.)

Signal Mountain town officials are shown beside the town's new $18,500 Ward LaFrance fire engine around the first of October 1959. According to Mayor Dodd, the purchase was part of an overall program to improve fire protection in keeping with the rapid growth within the town. Pictured from left to right are Commissioner Alfred E. Smith, Mayor Charlie Dodd, Commissioner Neal Bennett, assistant chief Russell Kell Jr., and Commissioner Earl Shaw Jr.

The Signal Mountain Golf and Country Club is a private club, but the town owns the club property. The first clubhouse burned, and the present one was built as a replacement. Over the years, improvements and upgrades have been made. It is the site for the majority of special functions by many of the organizations on the mountain because of the ballroom and beautiful surroundings. In 2005, a new pool was added. It is host to the annual Mountain Scramble, a benefit golf tournament for local organizations. Pictured from left to right at the 2005 Mountain Scramble are Tara Linehart, chairman of the event; Scott Hare, general manager of the club; and Karlette Baker, Mountain Education Fund chairman. The Mountain Education Fund was the recipient of that year's tournament. (*Signal Mountain Mirror.*)

Halfway between the Shoal Creek Road cutoff and the traffic light, on the right side of the road, stands a marker identifying Coolidge Parkway. This 26-acre tract of land was a generous gift to the town by Mr. and Mrs. Z. Cartter Patten in 1945 to honor military personnel from Signal Mountain. The parkway was named for Signal Mountain soldier and hero T.Sgt. Charles H. Coolidge. Standing at the sight of the marker on August 9, 1945, are, left to right, Addie Marr, Lena Givens, Bart Leiper, Mack W. Moore, J. Tom Allison, and J. Tom Gutherie. Sixty-two years later, Coolidge, seated in the wheelchair in the center of the photograph at right, is still honored, as seen here at the dedication of a Blue Star Memorial Marker in April 2007, where he was recognized as a special guest. (Signal Mountain Community Guild Archives.)

Built in the early 1970s, this pool is part of the Paul Mathes Community Center at the town hall. At the time, there was only one pool, which was located behind the Signal Mountain Golf and Country Club and was not large enough to be home to a swim team.

Today the Signal Mountain Swim Club, known as the "Green Giants," is a competitive swimming/diving team that is open to children and teens from all over the mountaintop. From left to right in June 2006 are the following: (kneeling) Adam Pickett, Anna Althaus, and Joshua Pickett; (seated) Katie Weldon, Connie Brown, and Tracy McHugh; (standing) Ben Leiper, Luanne Culpepper, Joy Tucker, Deborah Mynatt, Janet Pickett, and Leigh Althaus. (*Signal Mountain Mirror.*)

In the 1950s, the recreational board had plans for a new pool, four tennis courts, a playground, and two baseball fields. The town was then able to begin offering a more extensive summer program for children in the late 1950s. With the addition of the new town center in the early 1970s, the program expanded. Today, at summer day camps, children in kindergarten through second grade are offered arts and crafts, kickball, soccer, relays, games, group singing, rope jumping, and swimming instruction. While children in grades three through five are in the Junior Adventure Camp, they enjoy tennis, softball, basketball, volleyball, crafts, weekly contests, kickball, special events, and more. The camp is also a great summer job for young teens from the town. This picture is of one of the ballparks at the community center at town hall.

The current town hall was built in 1972 and remodeled in the early 1990s. The original charter called for a mayor and commissioners to run town business. In 1991, the charter was changed, and the town began using a town council form of government with a town manager. Jim Althaus was the first mayor under this form of government. He is pictured below on the left with council members Rachel Bryant and Bill Leonard (in back) at Mayor Althaus's last town council meeting in January 2003. Boards, commissions, and committees appointed by the town council conduct the business of the town with the council's approval. The town-hall property not only hosts the offices for the staff and a large room for town council meetings but is also home to the Signal Mountain Police and Fire Department.

The first Signal Mountain Public Library opened on October 17, 1970, in the building that was formally the first post office. The minister of the Signal Mountain Presbyterian Church, Dr. Gene Randolph, worked very hard with numerous volunteers to start this library for the citizens. Betty Driver Kistler was appointed the first town librarian.

Two years later, Margaret Spittler was named the first paid librarian. In 1972, the town bought an old house in order to expand the facility. In April 2007, Margaret Spittler was awarded Woman of the Year by the Signal Mountain Community Guild in honor of her service as the town librarian. Pictured from left to right are Helen Gates, Marjorie White, Margaret Spittler, and Sudie Thorpe. (*Signal Mountain Mirror.*)

The Friends of the Library was organized in 1980. They raised funds from dedicated patrons, and on February 29, 1988, a beautiful new building was opened. This structure was designed by Carroll Henley of Derthick, Henley, and Wilkerson at a cost of about $450,000. Connie Pierce (standing at podium) served as the town librarian for 15 years. She was instrumental in starting many programs, including Storytime, a once-a-week program for preschool children. In 2007, Pierce resigned, and Karin Glendenning (sitting in the chair) became the new town librarian. The Signal Mountain Library is a department of the Town of Signal Mountain and is central to the community. Book reviews, book clubs, writers groups, summer reading programs, guest speakers, and the Book Nook bookstore are all popular with residents. (*Signal Mountain Mirror.*)

The Mountain Arts Community Center (MACC), a department of the town, offers classes in arts, music, health and wellness, pottery, and dance from September through May, with SummerFun Camps scheduled from June through early August. The First Annual WinterFest, held in 2005, was a huge success thanks to the Town of Signal Mountain, Friends of MACC, the MACC board, FSG Bank, First Tennessee Bank, and a grant from Allied Arts. The Signal Mountain Lions Club, which meets at MACC, has partnered up with the center over the years by providing hot dogs and chili. Performing at the Winterfest are the Bandana Babes, a group of local women who sing and perform for fun. Down front are Amanda Cauthen (left) and Imogene Konvalinka. Behind them from left to right are Anne Thomas, Gay Burns, Anne Rittenberry, Emily Brown, Peg Willingham, and Margaret Ann Bentley. (*Signal Mountain Mirror*.)

The Annual Christmas Tree Lighting for the Town has become a tradition at MACC where fun, food, activities, and caroling make the evening special for children of any age. The Signal Mountain Newcomers and the Mountain Business Association have both shared the responsibilities for this special event. A highlight for the children is the arrival of Santa Claus on a Signal Mountain fire truck. Ray and Colleen Laliberte of Skwalking Heads, a very talented family, also make a significant contribution to the success of the programs offered at MACC, including producing and directing a children's play at Christmas. In addition, MACC is home to the winter production of the Signal Mountain Playhouse. Pictured is the auditorium at MACC filled with families singing Christmas carols. The current director of MACC is Karen Shropshire.

The Mountain Arts Community Center on 809 Kentucky Avenue was formerly Signal Mountain Elementary School. Today MACC is a community center proving a home for civic and community organizations. In 2000, MACC was recognized by the National Register of Historic Places. It is open to everyone and is available for community events or activities, including birthday parties, organization meetings, ball leagues, and scouts. (Karen Shropshire.)

As the saying goes, "We did not inherit this earth from our parents; we are merely borrowing it from our children." These words prompted Louise Mann and a group of volunteer citizens to create Recycle Signal in 1989, which grew into a partnership with the volunteers and the town. The new facility opened in 1991. Pictured is the attendant's building, a 110-year-old tobacco barn. (Loretta Hopper.)

The Signal Mountain Recycle Center is located on the west side of Ridgeway Avenue north of town hall. Items are collected four days a week, 10 hours a day. Beginning in February 2004, hazardous household materials were accepted. Once a month, these materials are hauled off to the city of Chattanooga, and according to Loretta Hopper, head of the public works department, the truck is always full.

In 2006, the recycle center was opened up to the general public for use by all citizens on the mountaintop. Families, students, and organizations contribute to the success of the center. One full-time and two part-time employees are often assisted by one or more temporary employees due to the popularity of the center. Pictured from left to right on a busy Saturday are Matt Hopper, Claude Griffith, Bob Lowery, and Timothy Thomas.

In January 1966, the Signal Plaza Shopping Center opened. The development was done by Windborn B. Willingham and Larry McGregor. The original tenants were M&J Supermarket, U.S. Five and Dime Store, Ralph's Coiffures, the Drug Shop, the Town Shoppe, the Prissy Hen, American National Bank, and Moccasin Realty. Ralph Smith, owner of Ralph's Coiffures, remained the longest—through 2007. This photograph shows an overhead photograph of Signal Plaza. (Frank Powell.)

Signal Crossing was developed across the street from the Signal Plaza Shopping Center when Signal Crossing Associates bought the land from Winborn "Windy" Willingham Sr. in 1984; in 1989, Signal Crossing II was added. Rick English was managing partner at the time. The original tenants were Revco and Brow Gallery, owned by Connie Blunt. Windy Willingham's grandchildren bought the center back from a predecessor in 1997. An artist's rendition of Signal Crossing is pictured. (Frank Powell.)

Suntrust Bank (American National Bank) constructed their building in the 1980s. The current Citizen's Bank location was originally an Exxon station, then a Hardee's restaurant. Ashley Plaza (originally Windy Ridge) was developed in 1992 by Winborn Willingham Sr. and Ann Rollinson, his daughter, and was sold in 2001. This picture shows all of these buildings, the First Tennessee Bank building, and the most recent addition, McDonald's, built in 1996. It also shows the Shell station in front of Pruett's. The second picture was taken in the late 1970s, when the gas station was first built. At the time, it was an Amoco gas station. (Frank Powell.)

In 1978, the M&J Supermarket (Mulky and Jackson) built a stand-alone store next to the Signal Plaza Shopping Center. The grocery store was bought by Pruett's Food Town in 1979. This picture shows how the grocery store looked when it opened, with a cedar shake roof, windows along the front, and a wide covered porch that greeted customers. (Frank Powell.)

This picture was taken in 1978, when the new stand-alone grocery store opened in Signal Plaza Shopping Center. Some of the employees stand outside the store waiting for customers. (Frank Powell.)

The Santa Train is a miniature train designed by Stanley Crewe and fellow carpenter Glenn Showalter. Many donations and volunteer hours from individuals and local organizations, including Rudd Montgomery of Push Hard Lumber, have made this annual display special to all on the mountaintop. First appearing at Christmas 2003, each year a new surprise is added. In 2006, a police car in honor of the Signal Mountain Police Department was added. Pictured from left to right at the unveiling are Mayor Paul Hendricks, police chief Boyd Veal, Glenn Showalter, and Stan Crewe. This year, friends of the Santa Train mourned the loss of three people deeply involved in the success of the train: Anne Ozburn; Susan Showalter, Glenn's wife; and the creator of the Santa Train, Stanley Crewe. Pictured below is the Santa Train complete with an evergreen forest, the newest addition. (*Signal Mountain Mirror*.)

Six

PEOPLE

Walter Marr is credited with building the first Buick car. He began working with David Buick in 1904. When Marr and David Buick's son Thomas test-drove the first car, known as the Flint Car, it was such a success that Buick car sales soared. In fact, Buick sales were so great that the Flint Car is credited as the car that built General Motors. Marr began working on the two-cylinder, valve-in-head engine and became the chief engineer. He liked the area so much he decided to make it his permanent home when he retired in 1912. He first lived at 136 Signal Point Road, called It Suits Me, while he waited for Marr Crest to be built on the street he named Flint in honor of his home in Michigan. He is pictured second from right with his family and personal fleet of Buicks. (Sarah and Bill Close.)

One example of the grand houses mixed in with the smaller bungalows built around the Signal Mountain Hotel is Marr Crest, built in 1928 for Walter Marr. This early photograph shows the beauty of the marble and brick home that was constructed of all fireproof materials. The two-story Renaissance Revival house is embellished with pan tile roofing, arches, and porches. (Sarah and Bill Close.)

Mr. and Mrs. Walter Marr (Addie) left a legacy of love for the town of Signal Mountain. Marr Chapel was built in 1932 by the Marrs. The oldest church in town, the chapel remains the same as it was when originally built. (Dot Shellabarger.)

Walter Marr (left) was married to Abbie Farrar Marr (right). In 1938, they hosted a party in honor of Lena and Claude Givens (center) at Marr Crest. The original site for their home was to be on a hill opposite the final site known as Marr Hill, but due to a recession it was not used. Marr Crest is made of marble and mountain stone. It was not built to Marr's satisfaction, so he had it torn down and rebuilt, using the first material for the drive and walkways. According to Marr's granddaughter, Anne Ballard, it was not uncommon for various dignitaries to visit the Marr family. It is said the man on the left riding horses with Marr and his son is Charles E. James. Walter Marr died in 1941. (Anne Ballard.)

Walter Marr's daughter, Olive Marr Mathes, made a gift to the town in memory of her husband, Paul Mathes, who died in 1965. With this gift, the town built the Paul Mathes Community Center in the early 1970s, which included the town hall, a gym, and a new swimming pool. At the time, Olive and Paul's daughter, Anne, was married to James E. Ballard, who was serving as a commissioner. James E. Ballard was instrumental in getting the community center built. His daughter Olive "Lolly" Marr Durant (Mrs. Daniel) is also active in the community. A well-known potter and art teacher, she has volunteered hours at the Mountain Arts Community Center in the town. Pictured in front of the Mathes Community Center is Evie Marr Durant with her grandmother, Anne Mathes Ballard, and mother, Olive Marr Ballard Durant.

Before becoming a U.S. senator in 2006, Bob Corker grew up in Signal Mountain attending Signal Mountain schools. He went to the University of Tennessee, Knoxville, and graduated in 1974 with a degree in industrial management. He credits a mission trip to Haiti with his father, Phil Corker, a former mayor of Signal Mountain, for teaching him the lesson of giving to others and the decision to create his own company, Chattanooga Enterprise, a nonprofit organization that helps people secure affordable housing. After being appointed Tennessee's administrator of finance and administration in 1994, he was elected mayor of Chattanooga in 2004. Bob and his wife, Elizabeth, have two college-age daughters, Julia and Emily. Pictured with Senator Corker (left) are his parents, Phil and Jean Corker. (Mrs. Phil Corker [Jean].)

Judge Frank Wiley Wilson and his wife, Helen, moved to Signal Mountain from Knoxville in 1961 with their two sons when Judge Wilson was appointed to the U.S. District Court for the Eastern District of Tennessee, Southern Division, by Pres. John F. Kennedy. Immediately after being sworn in, his knowledge of the law, his keen powers of observation, his quick, clear mind, and his innate sense of justice became apparent to members of the bar and litigants alike. Within three years, he was tested as judges seldom are by being assigned the difficult task of conducting the Jimmy Hoffa jury-tampering trial. Later he enforced federal mandates requiring desegregation in the public schools. (Helen Wilson.)

This picture was taken at Christmas 1962, when Judge Frank W. Wilson and his family moved to Signal Mountain. From left to right are Judge Wilson, Frank Carl Wilson, Helen Elizabeth Warwick Wilson, and William Randall Wilson. Making their home on Stratford Way, the Wilsons were active in the community and their church, Signal Crest United Methodist, where Judge Wilson taught Sunday school. They enjoyed camping with good friends Dr. Paul Nolan and wife, Anne, and Frank and Hilda Atkinson, who lived diagonally across the street from the Wilsons. According to Anne, one day she saw the Atkinsons' camper parked on Stratford Way and asked why, only to learn it was the FBI borrowing the camper to guard Judge Wilson and his family during the Hoffa trial. Judge Wilson passed away in 1984. His wife, Helen, resides in their family home. (Helen Wilson.)

Patrick Henry Thach was a Chattanooga attorney, born August 21, 1877, in Jasper, Tennessee. He was a special judge for circuit court judge Nathan L. Bachman. He was in the Tennessee State House in 1909, "when the liquor traffic was destroyed in Tennessee." This quote is at the bottom of the photograph of members of the general assembly of that year. He was the grandfather of Mary Scott (Thach) Norris, who penned this volume and reports that he never drank anything stronger than Hadicol.

Pat Thach and his wife, Jennie Raulston Thach, had three children. Their son Thomas Scott Thach was in practice with his father. Their daughters were Barbara Thach Varner and Jane Thach. Here Jennie (seated) is pictured at a luncheon with guests, from left to right, Mrs. G. E. Farmer, Mrs. Edward W. Windle (Peggy), Mrs. Volney Cissna, Mrs. Gene Kistler (Helen), and Mrs. Malcom W. Orr Jr. (Dot).

The Thach family bought and moved into this brick home, pictured above, in 1940. It had been built in 1925 by Mr. George Q. Adams, architect for the Signal Mountain Inn. Judge Thach was an elder at the Signal Mountain Presbyterian Church and taught the men's Sunday school class. In 1936, Thach was the Republican nominee for governor but was unsuccessful against Gordon Browning. He is pictured below in a three-piece suit milking his cow for a newspaper human interest photograph. (Dot Shellabarger.)

In 1961, Mrs. Claude R. Givens (Lena) was informed that a park on the mountain would be named the Lena Givens Park in her honor. This woman is probably the most influential person to shape the way the town of Signal Mountain looks today. A member of almost all the organizations on the mountain, she worked above and beyond the call of duty to make Signal Mountain beautiful. Pictured are Lena Givens (right) and Marian Dodd.

The mayor praised Lena Givens for her achievements, which brought much honor and recognition to the town of Signal Mountain. According to an article written by the late Irby Park, "Mrs. Givens was visibly moved by the tribute." Pictured from left to right at the site of the future park are Charles Adams, parks superintendent; Lena Givens; Mayor Charles Dodd; Sarah Lewis, president of the Improvement League; and Bud Bennett, park commissioner.

The huge sports complex at Shackleford Ridge Park in Hamilton County began construction in 2000. It is within the town limits and is considered the "Jewel of Hamilton County." In it are soccer fields, baseball fields, and miles of hiking trails leading to the Cumberland Trail and Prentiss Cooper State Park, which borders the park. One of the early pioneers to develop the trails was Sam Powell, pictured here on the left with Anne Nolan at the site of Nolan School on Sam Powell Road.

Sam Powell is responsible for laying out the Cumberland Trail. For many years, he has served as the chairman of the Signal Mountain Parks Board. He is considered an authority on all parks and trails throughout the mountaintop. Pictured is one of the many falls on the Cumberland Trail. (Sarah and Bill Close.)

In baseball, he was known as "the Tabasco Kid" and was a close associate of Babe Ruth. Norman Elberfeld played shortstop for several teams in the majors: the Detroit Tigers, the Washington Senators, and the Cincinnati Reds. From 1915 to 1917, he managed the Chattanooga Lookouts when they played on Andrews Field, before it became Engle Stadium. Kid Elberfeld and his wife, Grace, bought a home on Signal Mountain named Still Acres and raised their family of five girls and one boy. Their daughters, Nannie, Edith, Mirium, Dorothy, and Ruth, made up a basketball team called the Elberfeld Girls. The Elberfelds made Signal Mountain their permanent home. The Kid's baseball career covered more than 30 years. He died January 13, 1944, and Grace lived until 1961. (Chattanooga History Center.)

Mrs. Hugh Garner (Marilyn), at left, has been historical chairperson for the town since 1983. For many years, she and Roberta Bratcher and Brother Rupert, of the Signal Mountain Community of Alexian Brothers, collected and saved newspapers and other historical memorabilia, housing this material in the library to be later put in archival order. In the middle is Mary Scott Norris on the occasion of her retirement party from the library. At right is town council member Mrs. Jerry Robertson (Susan). (*Signal Mountain Mirror.*)

Artist Carolyn Wright (Mrs. Jim) is very well known for her lovely portraits and landscapes. She enjoys combining vacationing with painting. Her shades of color are vibrant and fresh. She is well loved on the mountain and never meets a stranger. Fortunate indeed are those who have her paintings. She is pictured second from left holding one in a photograph taken many years ago.

Claude R. Givens succeeded George O. White as mayor and served from 1951 to 1955. During his term, the town nearly doubled in population. An eight-man police and fire department with two modern fire engines and two patrol cars were added. New residents required new homes, so the development of Birnam Woods was begun. A long-range plan to provide sufficient water for residents was in place and included building a second storage tank. The treasurer at that time was Phil H. Stegall, and the commissioner was Charles E. Dodd, who succeeded Givens as mayor in 1955. Givens presided over the dedication of the Memorial Fountain on Armistice Day in 1956. He and his wife, Lena, will be long remembered as valued citizens of the town.

Seven
SCHOOLS AND CHURCHES

The Signal Mountain Grammar School was the first school in the town of Signal Mountain. It went from first to eighth grade. This picture was taken about 1928 or 1929 in front of the school. (John C. Wynne.)

The faculty at the Signal Mountain Grammar School is, from left to right, Pauline Seiters, principal J. Poke Dyer, Mrs. Smith Llewellyn (Liz), Mrs. F. E. Funk (Susie), Bernice Bailey, Maureen Howard, and Mary Baker McGee. This photograph was taken in 1933 or 1934. Susie Funk was the aunt of Signal Mountain resident Sarah Wilhite, who moved here to be near her aunt and who currently lives at Alexian Village. (John C. Wynne.)

This 1932 photograph was taken of all the students who were present every day of the school year at the Signal Mountain Grammar School. Pictured are, from left to right, the following: (first row) two unidentified students, Lois Hummel, Mary Sue Anderson, unidentified, Elizabeth Grayson, Mack Moore, and Deadrich Moon; (second row) Elizabeth Cunningham, Nancy Jane Moore, unidentified, Howard Brown, unidentified, Fred Grayson, and Alex Gamble; (third row) Dot Maupin, Weller Franklin, Hudah Brinkley, Geneva Brown, and Mary Jane Maupin. (Dot Shellabarger.)

This 1930s photograph of friends ready to go on a school outing to Nickajack Cave was taken just before they boarded the rickety old bus, according to Dot Maupin (Shellabarger), who is pictured on the far right. Also pictured, from left to right, are Mary Stuart Becking (McClain), Mary Nelle Hawk (Burke), Nancy Fitzwater (Goss), and Mary Jane Maupin. All five girls are still living on Signal Mountain. (Dot Shellabarger.)

This picture is of principal Ralph R. James and the first set of teachers in 1961 at Thrasher Elementary School, which is named after the late county executive Judge Wilkes T. Thrasher. Built around an open courtyard with native mountain stone, the building was designed by widely recognized architects Alan Derthick and Carroll Henley, both Signal Mountain residents. The new school cost $350,000 and opened its doors to 239 students in grades one through six.

The gym at Thrasher School is named the Dressler Physical Education Center in honor of Dr. Keith and Laura Lea Dressler, who were instrumental in securing the loan to finance the cost of the gym and whose children attended Thrasher School. Children celebrated the completion of the new gym in November 2005. Hundreds of residents and businesses worked along with the PTA for several years raising the money to build the gym. (Jean Trohanis.)

In 1975, Thrasher served grades four and five, but in 1990, it began serving students from kindergarten through fifth grade. Jean Trohanis, principal of Signal Mountain Elementary, was named principal at Thrasher. She was the first and only woman principal at both schools. Thrasher is consistently ranked in the top five schools in the state of Tennessee and is a National School of Excellence and winner of the Blue Ribbon National School of Excellence.

The 2007–2008 school year is the last for many teachers at Thrasher, including the principal. Many plan to retire. All these pictured have been on staff since 1999. From left to right are (first row) principal Jean Trohanis, Cindy Ezell, and Kelly Willingham; (second row) Amanda Cauthen, librarian Nancy Gill, Joy Gensheimer, Marty Roberts, Carol Floyd, Betty Julian, Faye Rothberger, Mary Tidwell, Cynthia Morris, and Karen Simpson.

Dr. Paul Nolan served on the Hamilton County Council (1966–1978), in the Tennessee House of Representatives (1968–1970), and on the Hamilton County Commission (1982–1998), where he served as chairman. He was also chairman of the Hamilton County Commission Committee for Health, Education, and Human Services. (Anne and Paul Nolan.)

Nolan Elementary School opened its doors in September 1999. The school was necessary due to the overcrowding at the other schools on the mountain. Bachman School was closed, as was Signal Mountain Elementary. Thrasher and Nolan became kindergarten through fifth grades and Signal Mountain Junior High became a sixth-through-eighth-grade middle school. Land owned by the Hamilton County Department of Education on Shackleford Ridge Road was chosen as a sight for the new school. Dr. Richard Casavant (left), Hamilton County Commissioner, stands with Anne Nolan. Pictured at the ground breaking is Dr. Jesse Register (far left), superintendent of schools. Next to him is Annie Hall of the Hamilton County Board of Education. Anne Nolan is in the dark sunglasses and pants suit, and her husband, Dr. Paul Nolan, stands next to her wearing a white straw hat. (Anne and Paul Nolan.)

The Hamilton County Department of Education and Town of Signal Mountain dedicated Nolan Elementary School in honor of Dr. Paul V. Nolan and Anne L. Nolan. Both served in many capacities to ensure all children receive a quality education. Anne Nolan served the town as both a commissioner (1979–1983) and mayor (1983–1987). She was honored as Woman of the Year. Through their public service, Paul and Anne Nolan truly exemplify what it means to be a good friend. Pictured in front of the mural of a knight on horseback, Nolan's school mascot, is the school principal, Ken Barker, with Anne and Paul Nolan.

Ground was broken on Saturday, June 14, 1958, for the new Signal Mountain Junior High School on Ault Road. Participating in the ceremonies are, from left to right, Mrs. Jack Bools; Ruth Allison; Raymond Forshay; Mayor Charles Dodd; school board member Roy Scruggs; contractor O. H. Raines; county school superintendent Sam McConnell; architect Gordon L. Smith; and I. A. Anderson, who was in charge of the program.

The music director at Signal Mountain Middle School (SMMS) is Robert Cirlot. The music program, with the largest organization sponsored by the school, includes sixth grade beginner band, seventh grade band, eighth grade band, sixth grade chorus, seventh grade chorus, and eighth grade chorus with about 225 students. The chorus and the band have both won awards at music festivals in several states.

As the youth community relations officer for the Signal Mountain Police Department, officer Greg Hill has assumed a position at each of the three schools in town. As the resource officer at SMMS, his job involves making sure the schools remain a safe learning environment for both students and staff. He already knows the youth at SMMS, having taught them the D.A.R.E. program when they were in elementary school. (*Signal Mountain Mirror.*)

Signal Mountain Junior High opened in September 1959 on a 14-acre tract. In 1990, the sixth grade was added to the junior high, and the school officially became Signal Mountain Middle School. At the end of the 2007–2008 school years, the doors to the school will close forever, as the new Signal Mountain Middle/High School is scheduled to open in September 2008.

Ground-breaking ceremonies in 2006 signaled a new beginning for students on the mountain. Pictured in no particular order at the ceremony are Lizetta Paturalski, Dr. Jesse Register, Dr. Jim Scales, Jan Ramsey, Signal Mountain mayor Bill Leonard, Walden mayor Elizabeth Akins, Dr. Paul Nolan, and Tom Caldwell.

Back in the 1950s, families began talking about a high school on the mountaintop. The Friends of Signal Mountain High School formally organized. With the support of Hamilton County commissioner Dr. Richard Casavant and Hamilton County board member Chip Baker, a high school became part of the county's plan.

In 2007, the decision was made to combine the middle school and high school, due to the fact that Signal Mountain Middle School was in disrepair and it would be more cost effective for the school board to combine the efforts. Eddie Gravitt was hired as the new principal. He is pictured in front of what will be the school entrance.

The firm Derthick, Henley, and Wilkerson Architects designed the new school. This is an architectural rendition of what the school will look like. The new Signal Mountain Middle/High School is scheduled to open in the fall of 2008 with grades 9 through 11. A 12th grade is expected the next year. Now residents feel the slogan "Complete Our Community" has became a reality. (Derthick, Henley, and Wilkerson Architects.)

For 11 years, Mildred Rothermel worked at the Log Cabin Church, located off Edward's Point Road. It was a mission of the Signal Mountain Presbyterian Church. She taught Sunday school every afternoon. In the summertime, she taught a Bible school for 10 days that ended with a program for families to hear and see what the children had learned. The bell in the steeple was taken off a train. It called everyone to the school. When she wasn't teaching at the Mission School, Rothermel taught Bible lessons to many children in many of the public schools on the mountain. She taught at the Signal Mountain Grammar School every Tuesday.

Eula Greeneway is pictured in the Jeep station wagon given to the mission school. It was used to take the children on rides or to carry loads of toys and supplies to families who came to the Sunday school or Bible school. Sometimes the station wagon was called a bus.

During recess at the Bible school, the children played games, including Poison Bean Bag, Jacob and Rachel, and baseball. Sometimes Mildred Rothermel would have a camp for the children where they would sleep over at her home. In the daytime, they went to class and studied the Bible; other times, they would go to the brow and have a picnic.

In 1929, Mrs. R. T. Faucett (Betty) and Mrs. D. A. Carruth (Minnie) decided to organize a church for the entire community. As a result of their survey indicating denominational preference, it became a Presbyterian church. The congregation met at the Signal Mountain Grammar School until 1932, when the Marr Chapel was built at 612 James Boulevard. The sanctuary for the Signal Mountain Presbyterian Church was finished in 1980. The Willet Stain Glass Studio, Inc., of Philadelphia, crafted the stained-glass windows. Dr. Frederick Woodward was the minister, and he wanted the windows to show mountaintop scenes from the Bible. There are four rose windows and 10 side windows.

A Sunday school class stands in front of the Marr Chapel of Signal Mountain Presbyterian Church. Pictured, from left to right, are (first row) Rom Mabry, H. T. Maupin, Charles Huneke, Bob Faucette, Jack Franklin, and John Goss; (second row) John C. Becking, James E. Lyle, Dennis Strickland, Tom Reynolds, Clifford Bowers, Lawrence Pickett, Billy Rogers, Hal Carruth, Mary Williamson, and Malcolm Williamson; (third row) Telfaire Brooks and Joe Wagner. (Dot Shellabarger.)

The great hall was completed in 2000. The youth wing was completed in 2006. It is affectionately called the Warehouse.

The charter members of Signal Mountain Baptist Church gather in front of the Signal Mountain Grammar School, where the first formal meeting was held on Sunday, November 3, 1946. Clyde W. Neely, a deacon of the church and publisher of the *Signal Mountain News*, is the man standing on the left. Members met in the school and purchased one lot at a time until they had enough land to build the church. (Leon Webb.)

Church members gather to lay the cornerstone. Kneeling in front is pastor Rev. R. W. Selman. Midway through construction, funds ran out, and Neely, also the church treasurer, wrote a letter to all the residents of Signal Mountain asking for donations. It was successful, and on Sunday, March 1, 1950, the Signal Mountain Baptist Church held its first service in the new building. (Leon Webb.)

Signal Mountain Baptist Church was only the second organized church in the town of Signal Mountain at that time. It is located on Ridgeway Avenue. The church added on in 1980 and again in 1998, when they built this beautiful new sanctuary.

Started in 1955, members of the Signal Mountain Church of Christ met in a temporary building on Signal Mountain Boulevard, but they moved into the handsome new church on Taft Highway made of native stone in June 1956. Leonard C. Johnson, who had been the minister for about two years, left in July with his family to do missionary work in Nigeria, British West Africa. Conrad Bates replaced him.

The interior of the Signal Mountain Church of Christ has the same native stone finish as the outside. The paneled walls surround the baptistery. The original building seated about 175. Today the church is expanding, adding a fellowship hall, new kitchen, and classrooms, due to a significant increase in membership.

The first meeting of the Signal Mountain Branch of the Chattanooga Stake of the Church of Jesus Christ of Latter-Day Saints was January 18, 1987. Some of the active families at the formation were the Donnie Burlinghams, Cathy Caughman and sons, the Peter Hansens, the Craig Harstons, the Kent Johnsons, the LaVon Johnsons, the Kerry Mays, the Harry Tritapoes, and the Dennis Wolfes. All could be called the "Pioneers of Signal Mountain Branch." (Deseret Ward.)

Pres. Phil Smartt of the Chattanooga Stake of the Church of Jesus Christ of Latter-Day Saints presided over the first meeting when the branch was organized. The first branch presidency organized at this meeting is, from left to right, Kerry May, second counselor; Reid Brown, president; and Harry Tritapoe, first counselor. There were 70 members of approximately 10 families at this time. The branch felt fortunate to meet at Thrasher School. (Deseret Ward.)

Ground breaking for the new chapel of the Signal Mountain Branch at the corner of Ault Road and Taft Highway was on March 26, 1988. The members met in the new chapel for the first time to see the general assembly from Salt Lake City. In 2000, the chapel was expanded to accommodate increased membership. To date, 24 have served as missionaries from the Signal Mountain Branch.

This picture of St. Timothy's Episcopal Church was taken in 1977. On February 14, 1952, a meeting was held at the Signal Mountain Grammar School to which all those interested in having an Episcopal church on the mountain were invited. The desire being evident, plans began to take form. The Reverend Joseph T. Urban was the vicar at the temporary chapel in a home on Cherokee Lane. (Betty Ewing.)

In 1953, Mr. and Mrs. Paul Mathes offered 8.5 acres of land on Mississippi Avenue for St. Timothy's Episcopal Church, the site of the present church, the rectory (built c. 1955), and the parish house (c. 1962). It was granted full parish status by the Diocesan Convention at Memphis on January 20, 1955. It then decided to expand by adding on to the parish house in 1968. (Betty Ewing.)

In 2005, St. Timothy's again added on. The mountain stone and stained-glass windows reflect the spirit of the remarkably active, energetic, and enthusiastic group of men and women who gathered that Valentine's Day in 1952. Their commitment has inspired following generations to continue building on the future of St. Timothy's. The rummage sales eventually developed into St. Timothy's Thrift Shop, a permanent project of the Women of the Church.

By 1955, the town of Signal Mountain had the Presbyterian church, the Baptist church, the Church of Christ, and St. Timothy's Episcopal Church. The only Methodist church was Fairmount Methodist, known as Signal Mountain Methodist but located in the Fairmount community outside the town limits. Pictured is that church as it was first established in 1857.

Members of a Women's Society of Christian Service night circle from Chattanooga's Centenary Methodist Church meeting in Signal Mountain expressed a desire for a church nearer home. On August 20, 1957, a new unit of the society was organized at the home of the Kay and Paul S. Pearces. The first worship service for the new church was held at the Masonic lodge on Signal Mountain Boulevard on September 15, 1957. In January 1958, worship services and Sunday school classes began meeting at the Signal Mountain Grammar School. On Palm Sunday, April 10, 1960, the congregation began meeting in their new church building on Ridgeway Avenue. On another Palm Sunday, March 18, 1969, the congregation processed into their new 450-seat sanctuary. The architect for this building was Carroll J. Henley.

Eight
ORGANIZATIONS

The Signal Mountain Improvement League—composed of members of the Garden Club of Signal Mountain, Garden Study Club of Signal Mountain, and the Signal Mountain Community Guild—along with three town commissioners—Mayor Charles E. Dodd, Phil Stegall, and Claude R. Givens—is responsible for erecting a fountain of weathered grey stone as a memorial to those from Signal Mountain in the armed forces who lost their lives in the service of their country in World War II and the Korean Conflict. The fountain is located at the corner of James Boulevard and Timberlinks Drive and was given to the town by Z. Cartter Patten. The dedication was held November 11, 1956. Twenty-one names are listed on the plaque at Memorial Park. (Signal Mountain Community Guild Archives.)

The Women's Community Guild was organized on June 6, 1928, at the home of Mrs. B. C. Crockett, who served as the first president. At the meeting on November 7, 1928, the name was changed to the Signal Mountain Community Guild. Its members, through volunteer service, are dedicated to community enrichment and preservation of human and natural resources in cooperation with other civic, cultural, education, and social organizations. During the next 20 years, the guild continued to thrive. The women of the guild and the Garden Club of Signal Mountain became a force to be reckoned with. Heading the receiving line is Mrs. Courtney Q. Nelson (Martha) at whose home on South Palisades Drive the party was held. With her, from left to right, are Mrs. Irby Park (Fay), Mrs. Elwyn Deakins (Margaret), Mrs. S. D. Ewing (Isabelle), Mrs. Fred J. Wagner (Mae), and Mildred Hall Nix. (Signal Mountain Community Guild Archives.)

Mrs. L. J. Morris Sr. announced plans for a tea for newcomers. This tea became an annual event. On May 29, 1958, Mrs. Claude Givens (Lena) was the guest speaker at the 30th Anniversary Community Tea. The general chairman was Mrs. Marvin Woodard (Betty), left, seen at the next guild tea in 1959. To her right are Mrs. L. J. Morris Sr. (Erma) and Mrs. F. H. Wiedman (Peggy). (Signal Mountain Community Guild Archives.)

By the end of 1949, the guild was still focused on service. It was at this time that the first telephone directory was discussed, as well as a fund-raiser to build an athletic site behind the country club. The Gahagan Fund had been created to provide assistance in education for the underprivileged children. The Book Club had become the Literary Club. Here members meet at the home of Mrs. Paul Mathes (Olive). (Signal Mountain Community Guild Archives.)

In March 1957, the officers for the guild were installed at the home of Mrs. L. J. Morris Sr. They are, from left to right, (first row) Mrs. Joel W. Richardson (Dorothy); Mrs. Charles E. Dodd (Marian), president; and Mrs. Edward W. Windle (Peggy); (second row) Mrs. John Spargo (Jane), Mrs. Frank B. Lightner, Mrs. A. J. Edgar (Vivian), and Mrs. Louise E. Ogle (Mary Katherine). The 1970s brought in a new wave of guild members. Meetings were no longer held in members' homes. Having received its charter as a tax-free organization, the Signal Mountain Family Center was completed and the Guild Room at the center became the meeting room for the guild as well as other cultural organizations. This room belongs to the guild and not the town and was redecorated for the first time in 2007. In addition, the Service Award was established to be given to a deserving student at Signal Mountain Junior High. (Signal Mountain Community Guild Archives.)

By 1960, the Evening Department of the guild was organized by Lena Givens. "Cuddy" Viall was elected chairwoman. After the ice storm in March, the guild members were ready to celebrate the annual tea, which was held on Tuesday, October 25, 1960, at the club. Prompt arrivals are, from left to right, Mrs. John Moreland (Mary Nell), Mrs. Bill McCool (Norma), Mrs. B. D. Gaddy (Ruth), Mrs. Robert Faber, and Mrs. Woodruff Banks (Marjorie). (Signal Mountain Community Guild Archives.)

The Signal Mountain Lions Club joined guild members to plan the annual Signal Day on Labor Day in 1960. Each department had an assignment. Pictured is Nellie Mae Rankin of the Evening Department at the bake sale table. The purpose of the event was to raise funds for recreational programs on Signal Mountain. (Signal Mountain Community Guild Archives.)

One purpose of the annual guild teas is to meet newcomers in the community. A Newcomers Department was established in 1979. In 1995, it became a separate organization. The Evening Department folded in 1982, was revived in 2002, and now is called the Evening Guild. The Literature Department of the Signal Mountain Community Guild is the last remaining department that was organized in 1948. The Literature Department meets once a month in the guild room. Officers and committee chairwomen for 2007–2008 are pictured, from left to right, in the Guild Room. They are as follows: (first row) Cleo Long, Pris Shartle, Norma McCool, and Helen Wilson; (second row) Adelaide Wigren, Helen Gates, Glenna Feller, Jane Parks, Shirley Byers, Dottie Walker, Nellree Berger, and Joan Withers. (*Signal Mountain Mirror*.)

In 1936, the Alexian Brothers bought the Signal Mountain hotel. It served in time as Postulate, Novitiate, Rest Home, Generalate, and in 1983, as a retirement community, Alexian Village. The Alexian Brothers moved their world headquarters from Germany to Signal Mountain, where it remains today. This picture was taken around 1984. (Auxiliary of Alexian Village Health Care Center and Inn Archives.)

The Women's Auxiliary of the Alexian Brothers Rest Home was organized November 5, 1950. The original objective was publicity. The first officers were Mrs. Edward Windle (Peggy), Mrs. George Seiters (Eve), Mrs. Harvey Hamilton, Mrs. William O'Malley, and Mrs. Joseph Wagner (Grey). For years, the annual fund-raiser to support these projects was a luncheon and style show. Glenn and Susan Showalter are pictured at the 2007 Caritas Ball benefiting the Alexian Village.

A Blue Star Memorial is "A tribute to the Armed Forces that have defended the United States of America." Sponsored by the Tennessee Federation of Garden Clubs, Inc., District III, in cooperation with the Town of Signal Mountain, a memorial marker was dedicated at the town complex on Saturday, April 21, 2007. The Blue Star Memorial Marker Committee chairwoman was Nellree Berger. Katherine Dowdy, District III director, welcomes over 100 guests at the ceremony. (*Signal Mountain Mirror.*)

In 1984, Betty Bonnard and Sue Henley received permission from the board of trustees at Signal Crest Methodist Church to use one of the rooms in the church as an office and pantry for the Signal Mountain Welfare Council. It was staffed by volunteers and supported by other churches in the community, and by 1985, there was enough money to support a part-time social worker, Helen Goldman, pictured at the 2005 Christmas Basket Day. (*Signal Mountain Mirror.*)

Aides to the 5th Region Scout Executive Conference are pictured from left to right on the grounds of the Signal Mountain Inn. From Troop 60 are (first row) Billy Magill, Scoutmaster Burton Franklin, and Weller Franklin; (second row) Jack Franklin, Joe Wagner, and Withers Howell. Joe Wagner, 91, is one of the oldest Eagle Scouts living in the Chattanooga area. Burton Franklin was the first scoutmaster for Troop 60. (Bob Wagner.)

Boy Scout Troop 35 from the Church of Jesus Christ Latter-Day Saints is gathered at a cave while on a camping trip. The current scoutmaster for Troop 35 is Neal Dexter. The Scouting program was organized on February 8, 1987. Harry Tritapoe served as the first scoutmaster. Today the church has a Boy Scout troop, Cub Scout pack, and a Venture Crew and is proud to have many Eagle Scouts from their program. (Deseret Ward.)

Boy Scouts are pictured at Philmont Scout Ranch and Explorer Base in Cimarron, New Mexico, in 1971. Troop 176 meets at St. Augustine Catholic Church. From left to right are (first row) Jimmy Russell; the Philmont guide; Bob Wagner, scoutmaster of Troop 176; and Russell Hill, Troop 116, Signal Crest United Methodist Church; (second row) Troop 176 members Harry Sibold, Brad Kidd, Ken Connor, Mike Fosbury, John Lions Jr., Pete Serodino, Mark Davies, and Jeff Albritton. (Russell Hill.)

The second group of Scouts to attend Philmont Scout Ranch and Explorer Base in Cimarron, New Mexico, in 1971 was also from Scout Troop 176, except Greg Leitner, who was a member of Troop 116. Sitting on the first row are, from left to right, Bill Lusk, Jim Lopez, assistant scoutmaster, the Philmont guide, and Mike Nation. Standing in back are Bill Nation, Jeff Nation, Greg Leitner III, Clay Walker, Chris Grabenstein, Steve Grabenstein, and John Reynolds. (Bob Wagner.)

The first scoutmaster for Troop 60 at Signal Mountain Presbyterian was Burton Franklin. A long list of men volunteered for this position between him and the current scoutmaster, John Glass. One was Ed Burke. He is pictured in July 1959 at Camp Cherokee on Ocoee Lake during summer camp. The picture was taken by Bob Wagner when he was in Troop 60, which was the only Boy Scout troop on the mountain at the time. Today Wagner is scoutmaster for Troop 176. In the second picture, Wagner stands on the far left in full uniform. Other Signal Mountain boys pictured include Ralph Hilmer, Gary Moss, Ken Gross, Robert Smith, Nick Norris, Billy Roberts, Dave Jones, Taddy Geiger, and Jim Fiaidly. In 1960, Troop 116, sponsored by the Men's Club of Signal Crest United Methodist Church, was chartered along with Troop 176 from St. Augustine Catholic Church to relieve overcrowding in Troop 60. The first scoutmaster for Troop 116 was John Alred, and Ken Tytula was the first scoutmaster for Troop 176. (Bob Wagner.)

Jean Blair Dolan (left), born November 12, 1915, in Worcester, Massachusetts, is pictured with her cousin, Norma Gray, in a photograph taken in 1926 when they joined Girl Scouts. Girl Scouts in the 1920s and 1930s wore merit badges on the sleeve of the uniforms, which were military-influenced khaki shirts with button-front jackets. Jean Dolan said Scouting taught her to "do a good turn daily." (Jean Dolan.)

Girl Scouts from Signal Mountain camp primitively in June 1956. Pictured at their tent are, from left to right, Lynda Wright; Sandra Keck; Gladys Hayes; and Ann Romick, assistant unit leader. (Moccasin Bend Girl Scout Council.)

The Signal Mountain Presbyterian Church hosted a special event in June 1955. Pictured are Girl Scouts and leaders from troops on the mountain. It is not known what the purpose of the event was, but Scout officials feel it must have been an induction ceremony where Scouts "flew" up from Junior to Cadette and from Cadette to Senior Scout. (Moccasin Bend Girl Scout Council.)

Today Moccasin Bend Girl Scout Council serves over 6,500 girls. Troops on Signal Mountain stay active with service projects, earning badges, selling cookies, and participating in summer day camp headed up by Lynn Talbot. Brownie Troop 33, made up of second graders from Nolan, Thrasher and Signal Mountain Christian School pose in 2006 in front of the mural in the Girl Scout room at the Bachman Community Center. Micki Hall (right) is their leader. (*Signal Mountain Mirror.*)

Girl Scout Troop 206 of Signal Mountain Presbyterian Church celebrates its third birthday in November 1957. Members of the troop include Patsy Bearden, Cynthia Beatty, Robbin Bohr, Janis Burke, Anna Callaway, Dana Eldridge, Margaret Ann Gibbs, Mary Gilleland, Annette Grand, Harriett Helton, Nancy Hillmer, Nancy Jo Hubbard, Jan Knox, Gay Lewis, Patsy Lines, Leslie Lyman, Mary Carol McAllister, Marjorie McClain, Gweneth Mack, Del Robertson, Faith Urban, Janice Walker, Rylie Ann Williams, Nancy Zeiser, Connie Chapman, leader Mrs. C. E. Burke (Mary Nelle), assistant Mrs. J. E. Gilleland (Helen), Mrs. J. E. Beatty (Faye), and troop committee member Mrs. J. N. McClain (Alma). Many of these young Girl Scouts still live in the town of Signal Mountain and are active members of the community. The year 2007 marks the 50th anniversary of Moccasin Bend Girl Scout Council. (Nancy Zeiser Sims.)

Mary Nelle Burke was the beloved leader of Girl Scout Troop 206 from 1954 until 1966. Girl Scouting actually began in Chattanooga in 1919, but the Chattanooga Council was chartered in 1926. It merged with the Cleveland Council and became the Moccasin Bend Council in 1957. According to Del Robertson (Mrs. Tom Francescon) and Nancy Zeiser (Mrs. Fletcher Sims), Mary Nelle Burke was the most kind and loving Girl Scout leader a girl could ask for. Janis Burke Speck, Mary Nelle's daughter, adds that over the years, assistant leaders came and went, but her mother was always the constant. Mary Nelle was married to Ed Burke, who was a longtime scoutmaster for Boy Scout Troop 60 at Signal Mountain Presbyterian Church. He is pictured below in 1967 in his uniform. The Burkes' home on James Boulevard was a common sight for both Boy and Girl Scouts. (Mary Nelle Burke.)

The Signal Mountain Lions Club was established on August 14, 1958, and was considered the largest club ever chartered in Tennessee. Ellis Smith Jr., Moss White, Joe Wagner, and Pat St. Charles are the only living charter members of the club. The official historian for the club was Irby Park (pictured), who was Lion of the Year in 1974. The first Fourth of July Fireworks and Barbecue sponsored by the Lions was in 1964. In 1968, the Lions joined with the Community Guild for the Signal Days, which became the Labor Day Barbecue. The barbecues support various organizations in the community. The Lions continue to support their own projects, the White Cane and Sight Services, as part of their commitment to site conservation. In addition, they offer scholarships to high school students and work closely with the Remote Area Medical in the Lone Oak Community. (Signal Mountain Lions Club.)

In 1969, "Chick" Thomas, the mayor of Signal Mountain came to the Lions Club meeting and asked Ellis Smith if he would set up fireworks after the next Fourth of July barbecue, as he had worked with munitions during World War II. Ellis (standing) agreed and did so with help of Moss White (kneeling) and his son Jim Smith, until professionals took over in 1993. (Ellis Smith.)

The Lions Club meets twice a month at the Mountain Arts Community Center and welcomes new members. They enjoy programs from a variety of people, including local celebrities, as seen in this picture taken in 2003. Pictured from left to right are Lion Travis Billingsly, Thom Benson and Jed Mescon from WRBC Channel 3 TV, and King Lion Ben Holt. (*Signal Mountain Mirror*.)

The Signal Mountain Playhouse was formed in 1972. The first show was *The Great Cross Country Race*. The first outdoor show in the current outdoor theater was *The Wizard of Oz* in 1975. In 1983, the first winter production, *The Odd Couple*, was produced. The playhouse is a volunteer organization made up of 24 board members and 4 youth representatives. One member, Glenn Showalter, has been involved from the very first and is a major player in all playhouse endeavors. This cast picture for *Lend Me a Tenor* includes, from left to right, the following: (rear) Jeff Buchwald, Janet McInturff, Eric Schubert, Travis Boles, and Rob Inman. In front are Christine Arnold, Pat Boles, and Chris Davidson. (Greg and Jeannie Forehand, Contemporary Portraits.)

Gov. Jim McCord (left) and Signal Mountain mayor George O. White (right) stand among the guests with Paul S. Mathes, and Raulston B. Lattimore, assistant chief of the U.S. Travel Division of the National Park Service, at the dedication of Signal Point Park on May 1, 1948. The three-acre tract was given to the U.S. government by the Signal Mountain Garden Club, private donors, and the town. (Chattanooga–Hamilton County Bicentennial Library.)

The park later became part of the Chattanooga–Chickamauga National Military Park. Elise Chapin is pictured at the unveiling of the marker. For two years, the Garden Club worked to get this project approved, and without the generous donation of land by Mr. and Mrs. Z. Cartter Patten (Elizabeth), and Mr. and Mrs. Pat St. Charles (Lucille), the park would not have been possible. (Chattanooga–Hamilton County Bicentennial Library.)

Charles E. James and his driver stand at the edge of the bluff just below the cliffs. He looks out at the Tennessee River and the surrounding mountains. He sees the magnificent view of the "Grand Canyon of Tennessee"—the Tennessee River Gorge, the deepest gorge east of the Mississippi River. Today this vantage point is called James Point in his honor. That day in 1912, he was most likely convinced that his decision to move to the mountain, build a hotel and a road up the mountain, and settle down with his family would lead to the birth of a town—Signal Mountain, Tennessee. (Chattanooga–Hamilton County Bicentennial Library.)

REFERENCES

Auxiliary of Alexian Village of Southeast Tennessee Health Care Center and Inn Archives
Boy Scout Troop 116, Russell and Lynn Hill
Boy Scout Troop 60, John Glass
Church of Jesus Christ Latter-Day Saints, Deseret Ward
Del Francescon
Derthick, Henley, and Wilkerson Architects
Dr. and Mrs. Paul Nolan
Garden Club of Signal Mountain
Greg and Jeannie Forehand, Contemporary Portraits
Janis Burke Speck
Jean Dolan
Jean Trohanis
Joe Wagner
Lara Caughman
Lookout Mountain Investment Company, Frank Powell
Mary Nelle Burke
Moccasin Bend Girl Scout Council
Mountain Gazette, Signal Mountain Library Archives
Mountain Post, Signal Mountain Library Archives
Nancy Zeiser Sims
Robert White
Sam Powell
Signal Crest United Methodist Church, Kay Pearce
Signal Mountain Baptist Church, Leon Webb
Signal Mountain Church of Christ
Signal Mountain Community Guild
Signal Mountain Lions Club, Phil Johnson and Irby Park Files
Signal Mountain Mirror, Signal Mountain Library Archives
Signal Mountain Playhouse, Anne Rittenberry
Signal Mountain Presbyterian Church
St. Timothy's Episcopal Church, Betty Ewing
Town of Signal Mountain, Loretta Hopper

Visit us at
arcadiapublishing.com

www.ingramcontent.com/pod-product-compliance
Lightning Source LLC
Chambersburg PA
CBHW081419160426
42813CB00087B/2350